From Where Grandma Sits: Bird Watching

"Kids of all ages"

Jessie Eldora Robertson

DEDICATION

I DEDICATE THIS BOOK TO MY FAMILY, JASON & Rhona, my grandchildren Angela & Jordan, and Brittany & great daughter Aria I also would like to include my Sponsored child, Mary, in Africa, who is now a young teenager; was my girl for over ten years and is now out of the sponsored system because her family is doing well. It was when I was writing letters to her, I wanted her to know about the birds that come into our yard. It was an inspiration to start the story.

"Even if the kids are small, they want to learn like big kids do." Grandma is outside in the summer months and the springtime. Actually, as soon as she does not have to wear a winter jacket. The visiting birds are the life around the yard. The visiting grandchildren, get to watch the birds with grandma. They share Grandma's pleasure in in listening for the birds' calls. They want to learn to see if they can recognize which bird, it is that they hear? But they only have a few weeks to learn before the summer holidays are over. Before going home, the grandkids get to see the 'big bird' the swans at the island park. Enjoy the humor in Birdwatching, in this story.

Enjoy this picture book all about the birds!

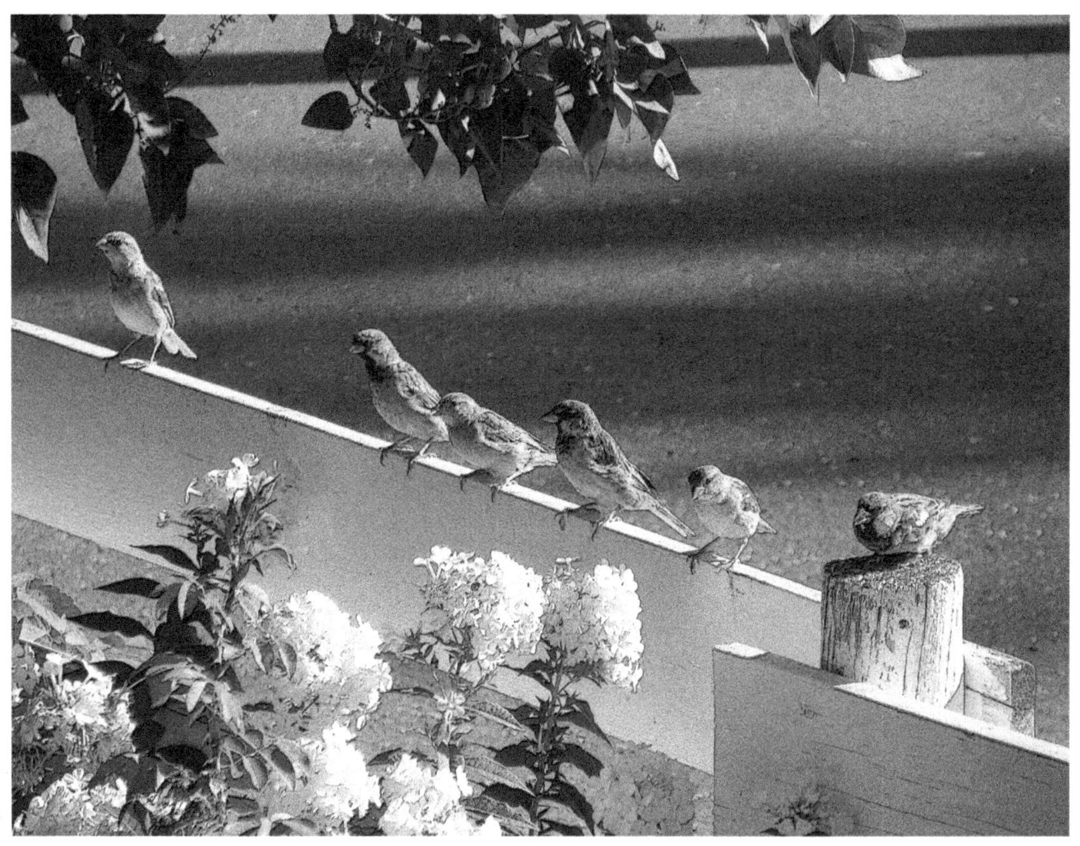

Can you tell which birdie House Sparrow is the smallest baby?

Contents

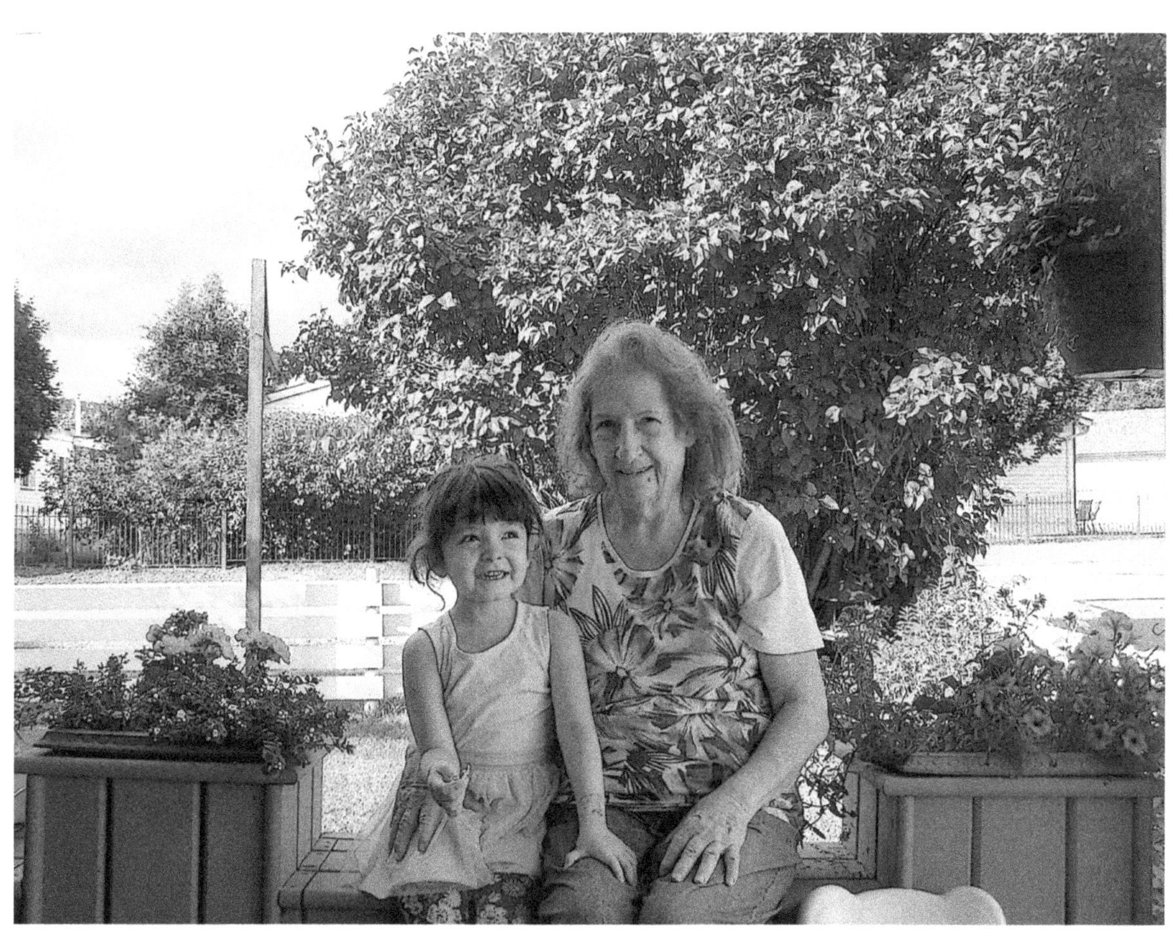

Aria and Grammy sitting on the porch deck

This BOOK BELONGS TO

____

What has 2 legs, 2 wings and a beak and feathers?

Chapter 1

Summer holidays at last

Grandma is rushing-out to the porch with her camera again. "What are the birds doing now?" Angela thinks. But today the weather is different there is smoky sky. Even if grandma looked out of her big glasses, the ones called binoculars, the birdies would not look good.

Angela is visiting grandma, together with her brother Jordon who is 3 1/2-year-old. Angela is seven. They visit their relative Aria, who is 3 years old. Aria lives with her great grammy, our grandma too. Summer holidays are the best! We love to sit on the porch deck, watching the birds. We get to eat ice cream! Sometimes grandma serves us all hot muffins.

Aria likes to look up to the clouds in the sky. Angela likes to walk around the colorful yard, and look at and smell the pretty flowers. Sometimes Aria helps grammy water the flowers. Aria really enjoys placing the bird seeds in the feeder. Jordan likes to stomp his feet on the dirt.

For all of us kids, our favorite thing is to watch the birds that Grandma is watching!

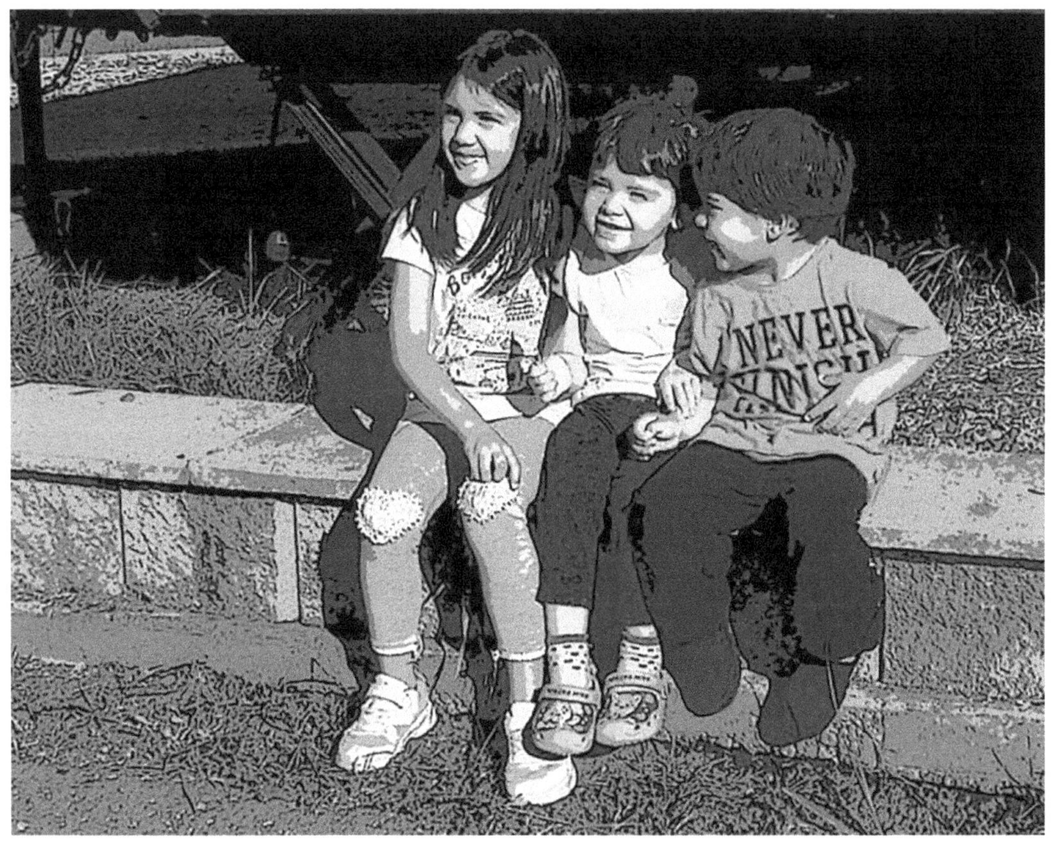

CHAPTER 2

The birds are pets, really

LITTLE BROWN BIRDS LINE-UP ON THE WHITE fence. The birds are near the bird feeder where there is water and bird seed. Grandma says these birds are called House Sparrows. They are the biggest flock of birds that come all year, except in the winter. In winter they disappear ... somewhere ... maybe under the eaves of the workshop. "Why, are there so many?" asks Jordon. "Sparrows have a least two families each year with the females laying three to five eggs at once," replies Grandma.

One thing every interesting about the sparrows is that the father feeds the birdies just like the mommies do.

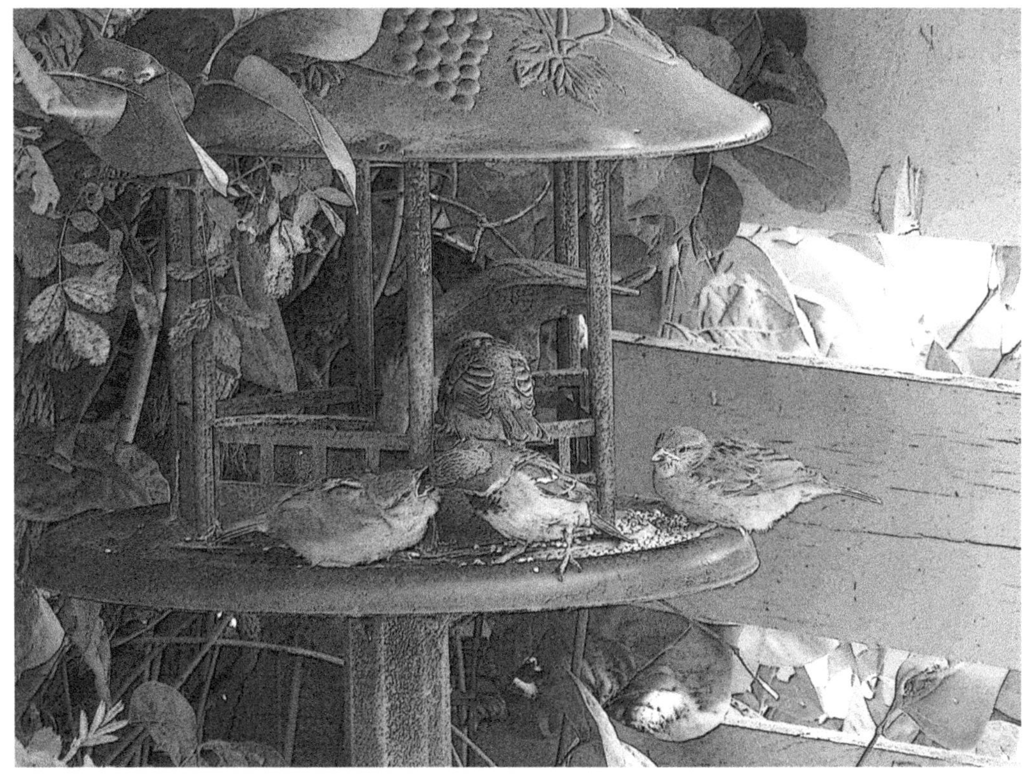

CHAPTER 3

More about the House Sparrow and the Bohemian Waxwing bird

GRANDMA WOULD LIKE OTHER BIRDS TO VISIT longer, there are pretty colorful birds that fly into the yard but do not stay. They just put-on a fashion show for a while. An early spring bird is the American Robin. "Well, Jordan pipes-up, they have a lot of yards to choose from." A bird who comes to the yard in the spring and stays a while is the sparrow's cousin, the White crowned Sparrow, he is just as noisy! Chirruping continually. It's just like one big happy family reunion. A second bird feeder was built in another tree for all birds. And then, another and another in the back yard.

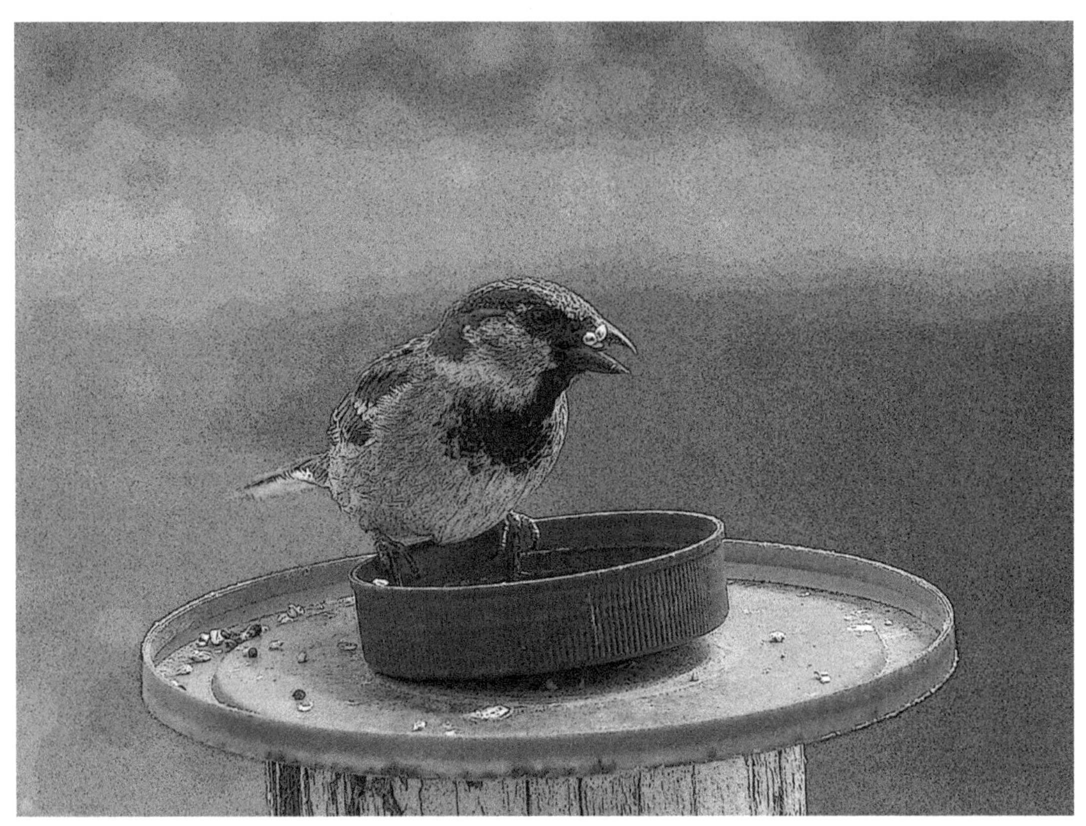

Male House Sparrow cracking the seed

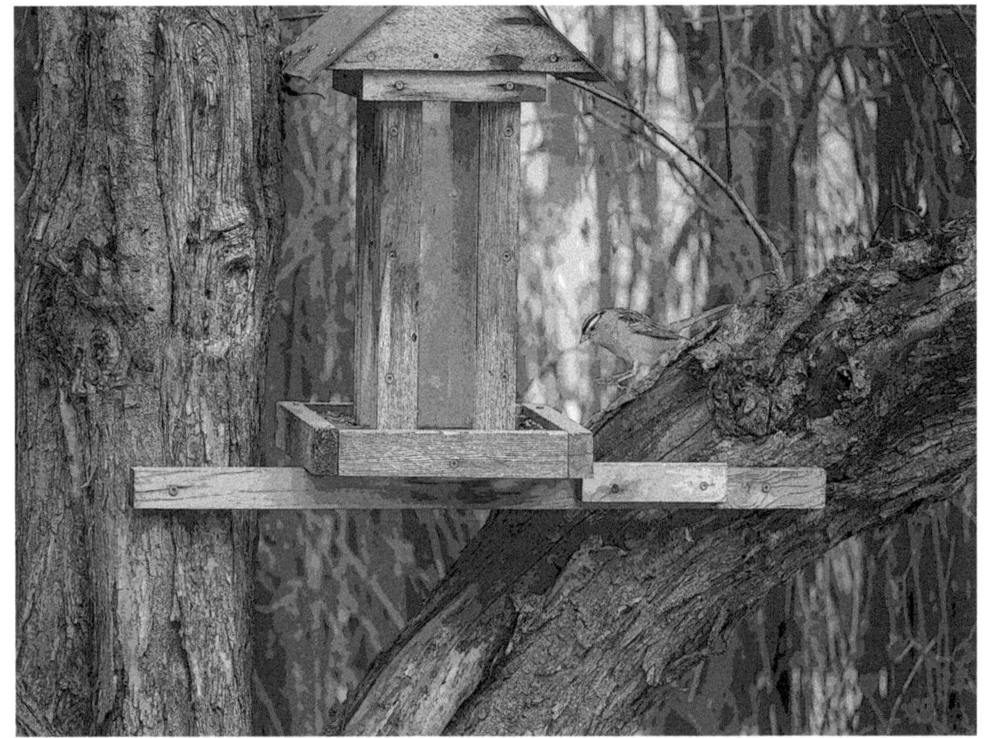

White crowned Sparrow landing in the tree

Grandma is happy when the House sparrows start circling the whole yard because they are less noisy. They perch, one by one on the fences around. "Look, look!" Aria cries out, "A sparrow is drinking from my water and sand play table! House sparrows are six inches long, their bodies are stout and thick. The male bird has a chestnut head, grey crown, white cheeks and a black bib. The female bird is not as colorful. The female has a buffy grey head, a tan eyeline, a grey underside and they have brown backs. There are 26 species of sparrows all over the world! Sparrows eat potatoes, corn, wheat, seeds, and insects. They chirp. "Cheap, cheap, cheap", they call. Jordon noticed when baby sparrows were on the electrical line, the call was pee, pee. The sparrows are very sociable, they like to know where each other are so, they get louder! Sometimes, the Bohemian Waxwing flock into the yard in great numbers.

The Bohemian Waxwing's numbers have increased due to ornamental plantings of fruit trees such as crab-apples and mountain ash, which provide the birds with a feast of fruit. Bohemian Waxwings are full-bellied, thick-necked birds with a shaggy crest atop a pin head. The wings are broad and pointed, like a starling. The Bohemian Waxwing is grayish brown overall with subtle peach blushing around its black mask. The wings have 2 distinctive white rectangular patches and red waxlike tips on the secondaries. The undertail is rusty and the tail is tipped in yellow. "Waxwings feed on the berries from the Ornamental Crab-apple tree" Grandma tells us.

Grandma says she thought she would want an Aviary – a large cage structure - where the birds can flock too; but she knows there are too many birds coming to the yard anyways.

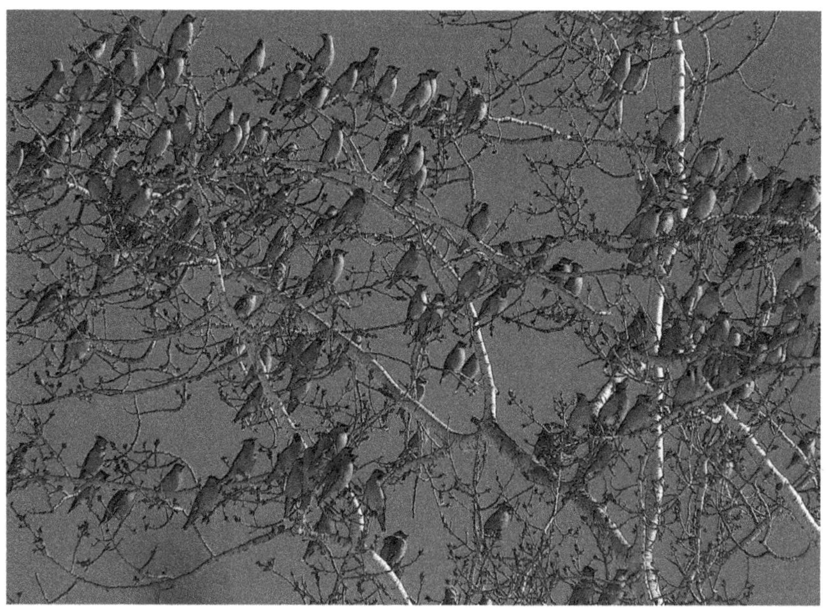

Bohemian Waxwings flock to the tree for berries

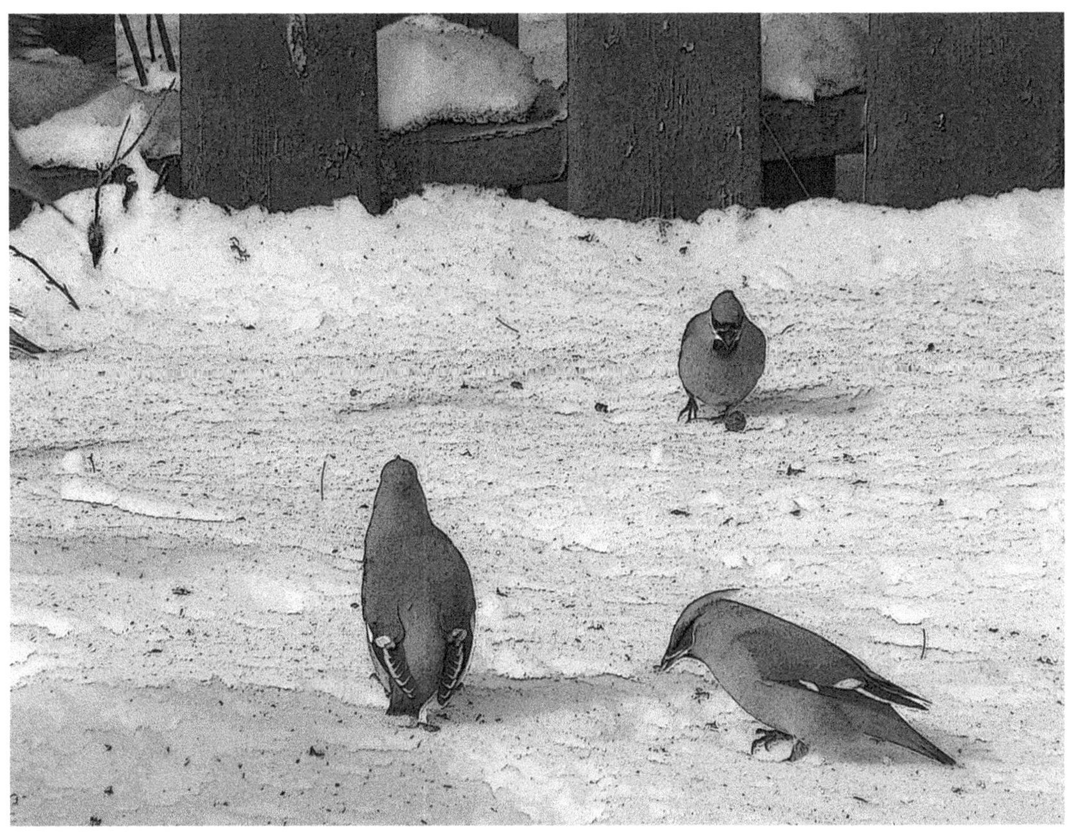

Bohemian Waxwings birds on the snow eating fallen berries

CHAPTER 4

Chickadee and the House Finch and the Junco

THEN ALONG COMES THE CHICKADEE, A BLACK capped Chickadee. A bird that is considered "cute" thanks to its oversized round head, tiny body, and curiosity about everything, including humans. The chickadee's black cap and bib; white cheeks; gray back, wings, and tail; and whitish underside with buffy sides are distinctive. This bird will share the bird feeder with the sparrows.

The House Finch is sometimes red, the male House Finch comes from pigments contained in its food during molt (birds can't make bright red or yellow colors directly). Molting is when birds lose their older, broken feathers. So, the more pigment in the food, the redder the male. This is why people sometimes see orange or yellowish male House Finches. Angela likes the stripped pattern of the feathers design.

Grandma forgot to talk about the Junco. Sometimes Junco, before, comes before the snow melts the comes before all the snow has melted away. Juncos make their home in woodland areas. They've got wings, but juncos prefer to hop around the forest floor, and Grandma's yard. They spend as much of their time on the ground. The birds 'puff-up' in the cold.

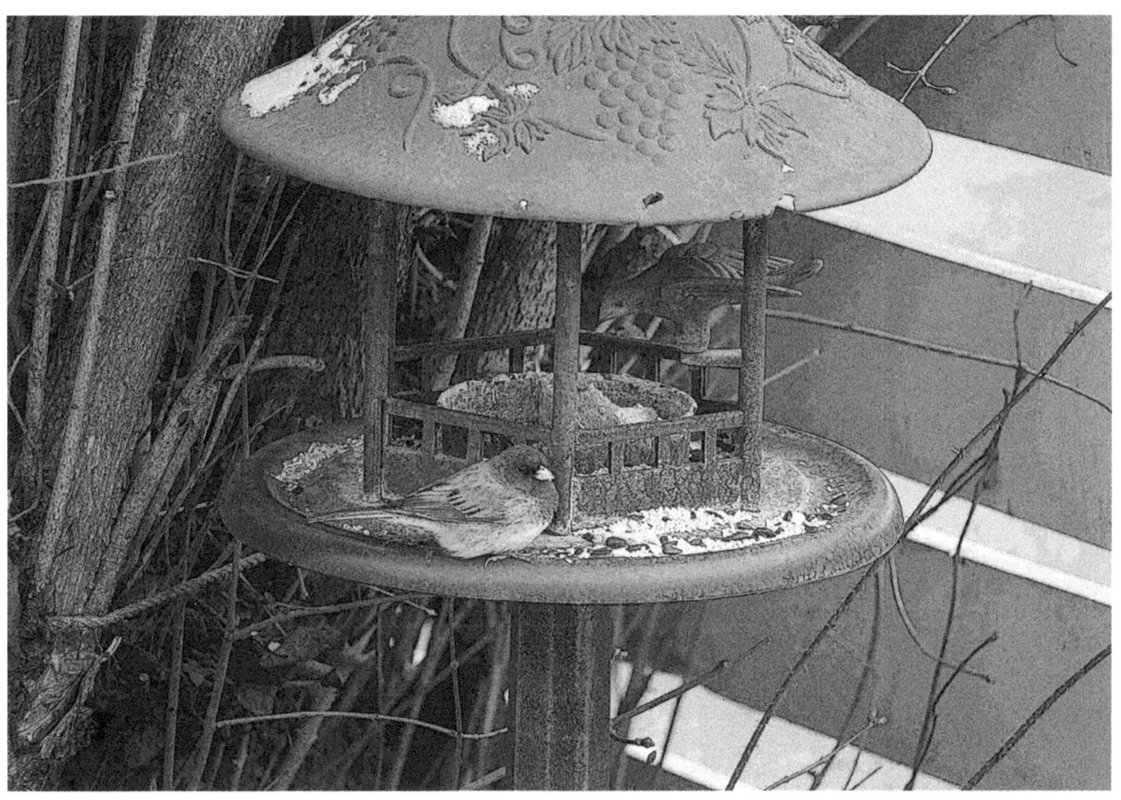

Junco bird in the snow - Can you tell which bird is the real one?

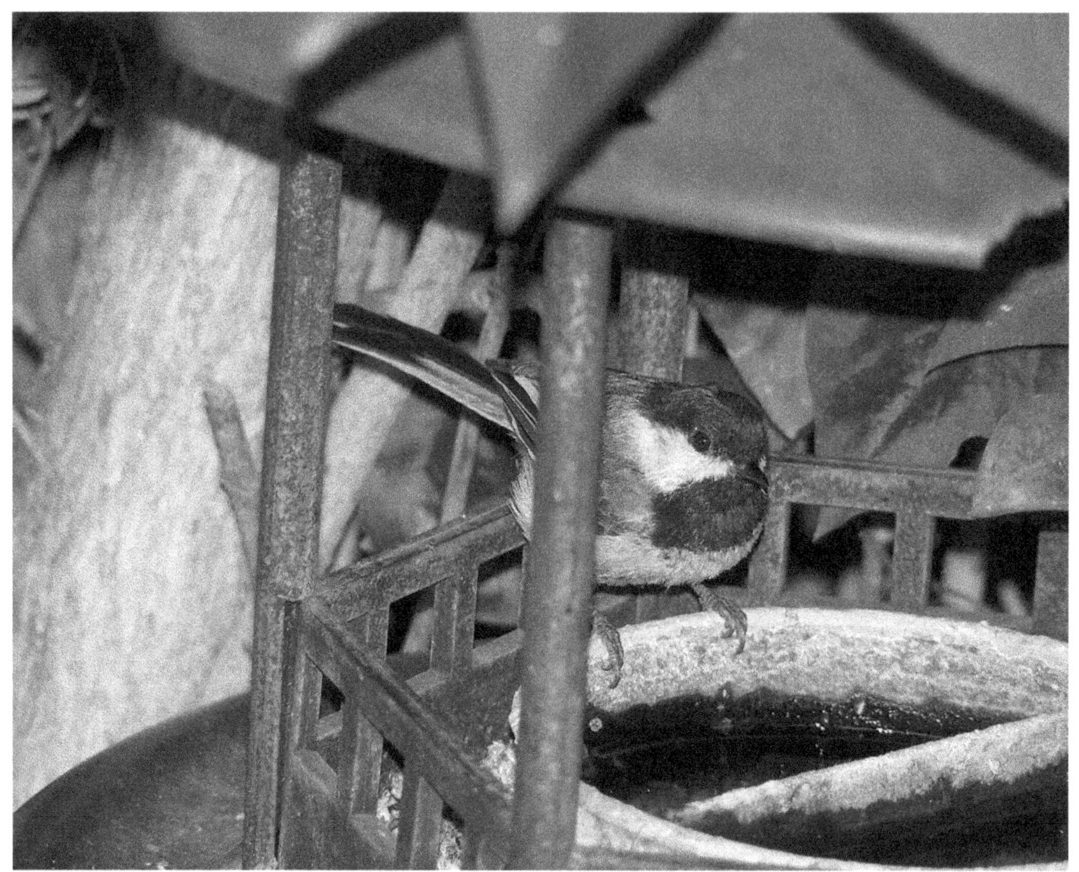

Chickadee in the birdfeeder

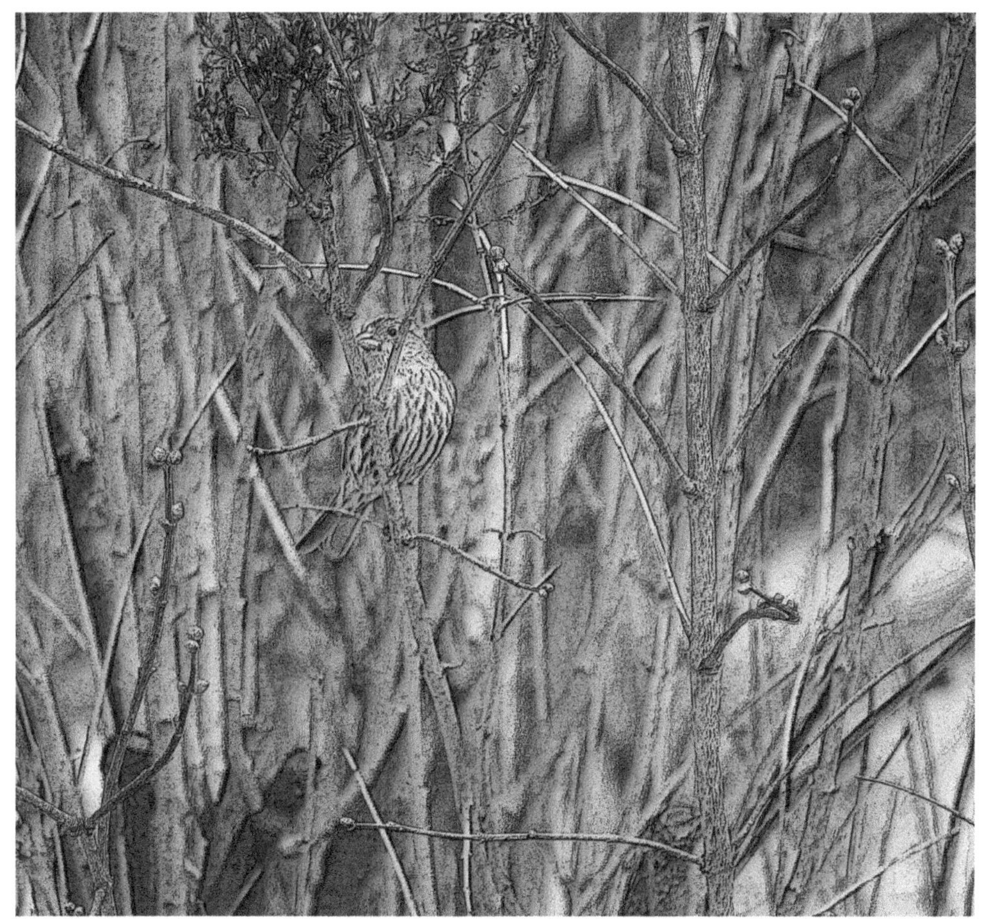

House Finch in the branches

CHAPTER 5

Those Crows, those pigeons, and that cooing Morning dove!

THERE ARE TWO OTHER BIRDS THAT ARE around the street, that can fly into the yard, they are the Black Crow and the Pigeon. Grandma considers those birds a big nuisance. The pigeons try to steal the little birds' seeds, and one of their bodies can fill the whole bird feeder. Grandma does not like it when the pigeons sit on the high wire of the electrical line and their poop lands on her car! Pigeons are grey, dark grey, grey with purple and brown. The crows walk on the steel roof of the house, and that makes a racket! Who are these crows anyways? What is that biggest black one sitting on the street? "A Raven," says Grandma, "it is not a crow. "I saw grandma throwing a green tennis ball up on the roof at the crows early one morning" says Angela, "but, she couldn't hit them". Crows have many voices, of course the "caw", but crows have many sounds because they can mimic, pick-up sounds around them. They can sound like a cat, or a baby crying!

"What's a raven?" all the kids shout. Ravens are highly intelligent animals and can use their beaks to rip objects open, helping them find both food and shelter. Ravens have bigger, curvier beaks than crows. Ravens have a crocking call, and are a talking bird. Grandma says that the Ravens are hardy around much.

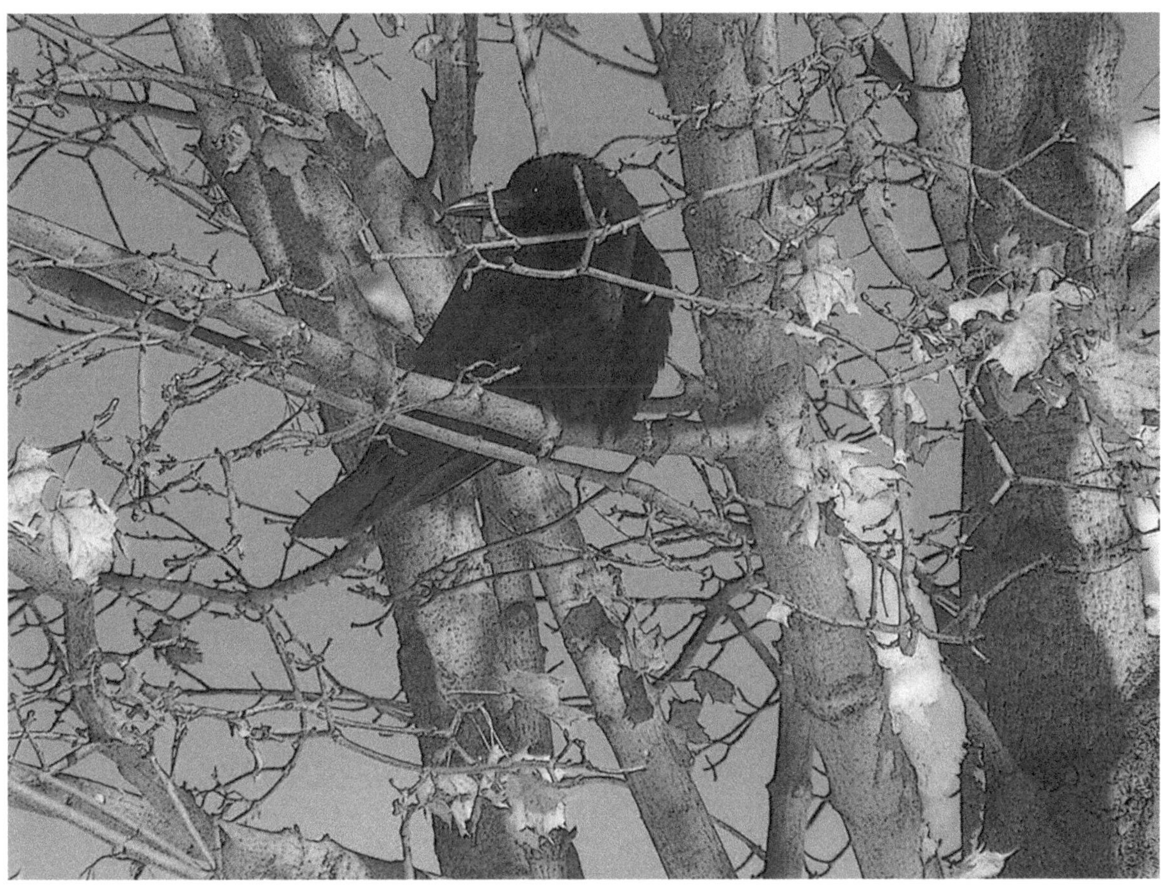

Crow

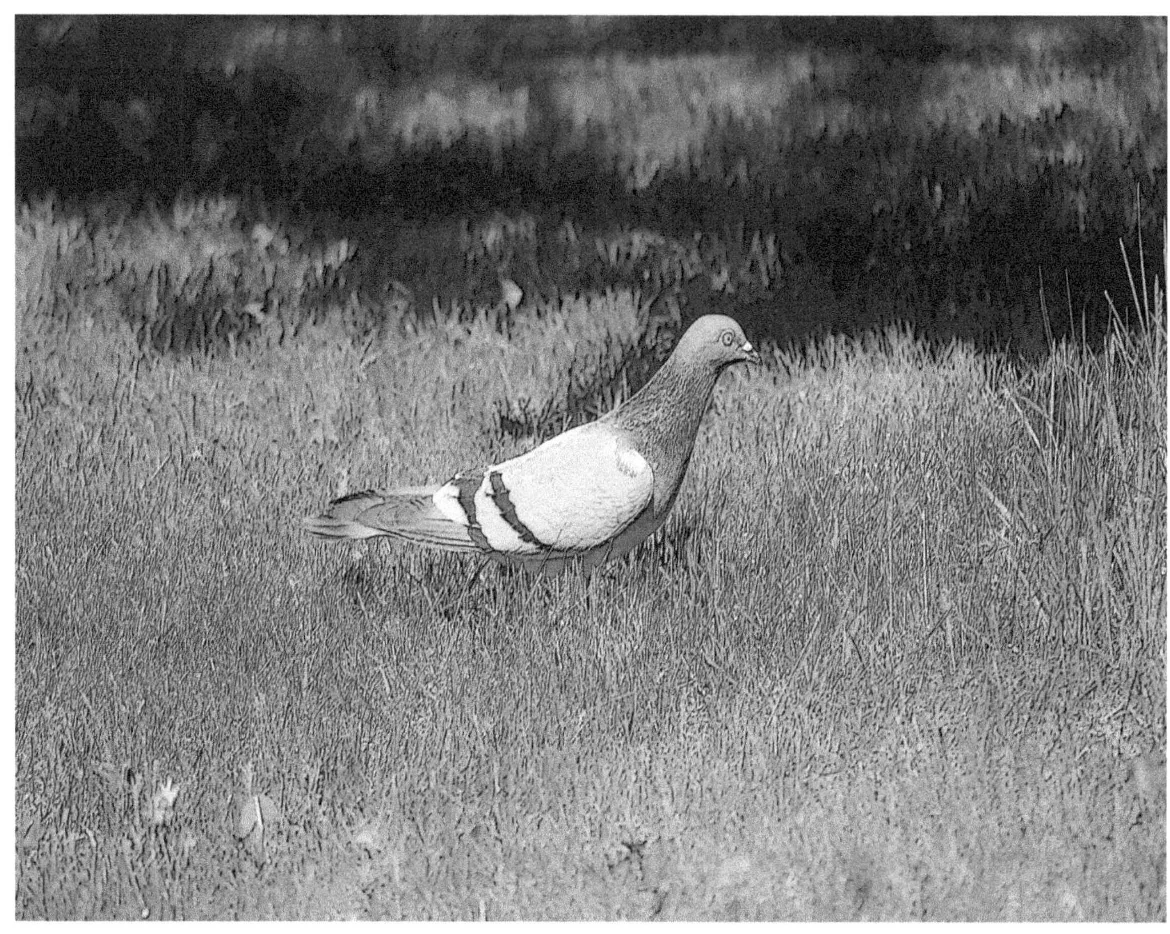

Grey pigeon in the grass

The morning dove is something else! Everyone knows by it's name that it coos in the morning but … we hear it cooing in the evening. The sound is haunting because it goes on and on, more so at night. Actually it isn't pleasant. It is actually called a mouring dove. That is why it is hauting! The bird has two different coos, and also twittering.

The morning dove looks much like the pigeon, but is a very light grey and white.

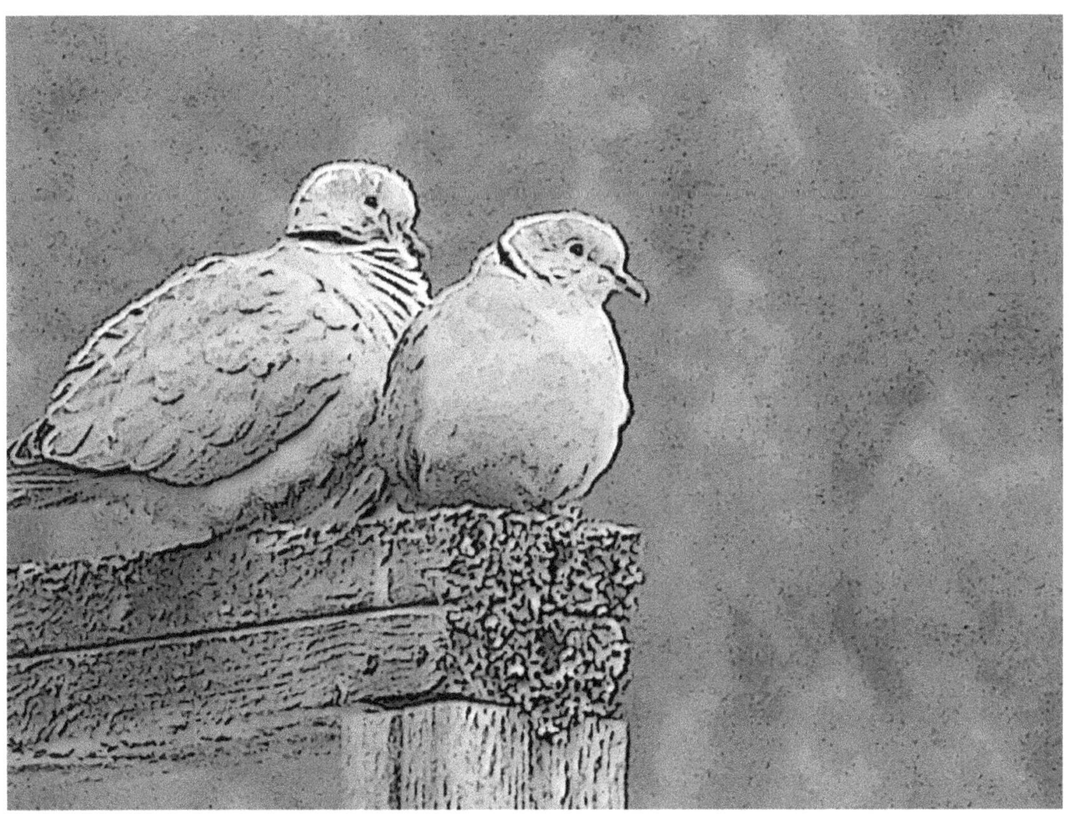

CHAPTER 6

Pretty Robins a sign of Spring and a colorful Woodpecker

THE NORTH AMERICAN ROBIN IS PART OF the thrush family, it's big, with a yellow beak and striking white markings around the eyes. Our backyards are a little like natural openings in forests, for which robins are naturally adapted. Robins are flexible enough to eat many kinds of food and nest in various situations. Robins lay tiny blue eggs.

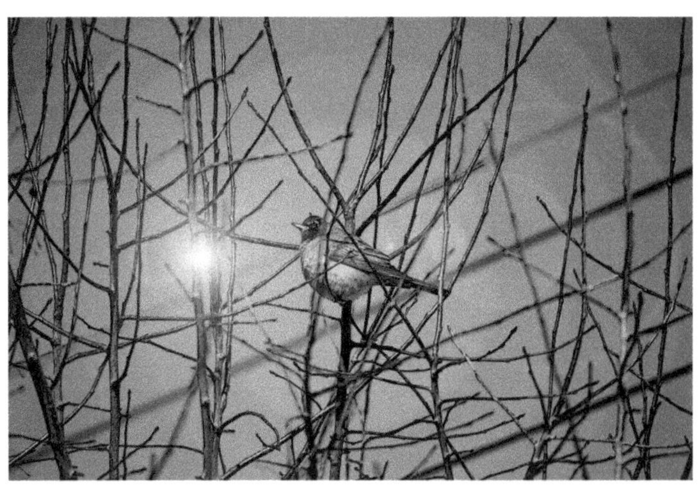

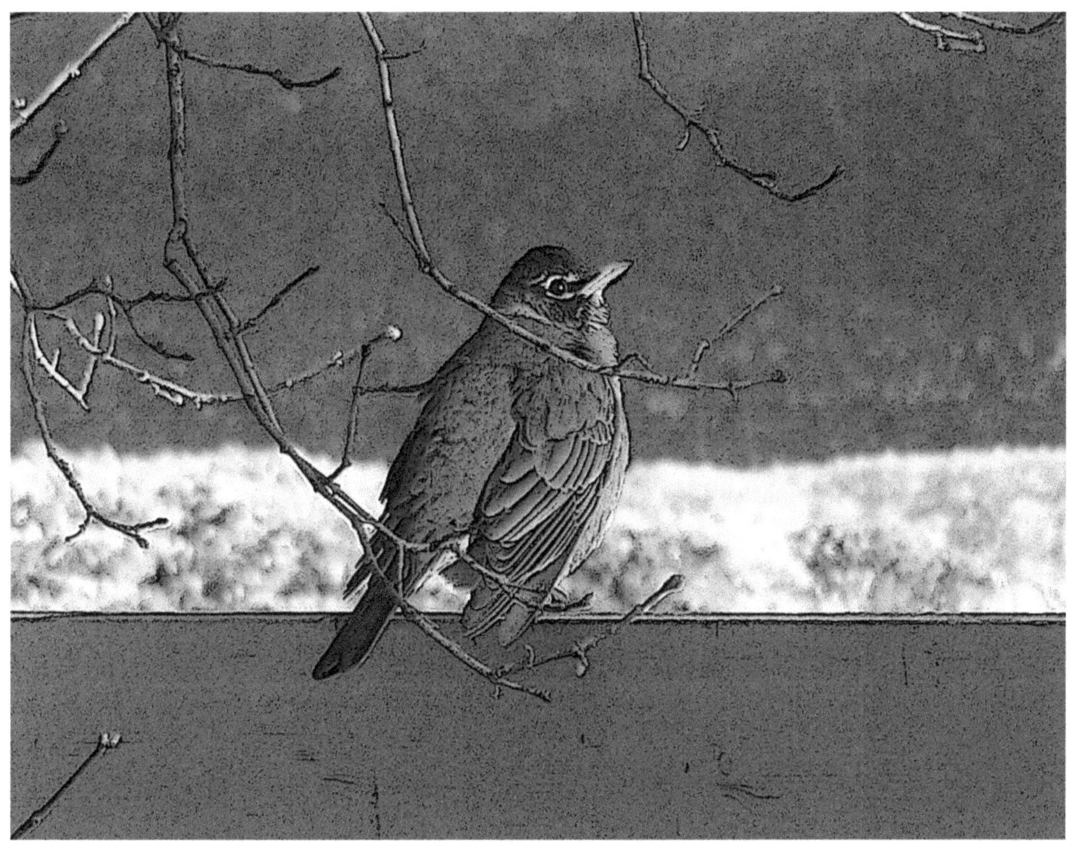

Robin on the fence in the early springtime

Can you see the snow?

Flickers' wingspan can reach 18 to 21 inches. Ever thought what an ant hill is good for, other than being a home for the ants? The Flicker will run a few steps and stop, run a few more steps and stop, until it finds an anthill. Ants are their most important source of food. And then, there are: raccoons, house cats that live in the wild, and hawks, that try to eat the Flicker! Actually, their nests are protected not only from destruction but also from disturbance. The bird can thank a pretty strict piece of legislation called the Migratory Birds Convention Act.

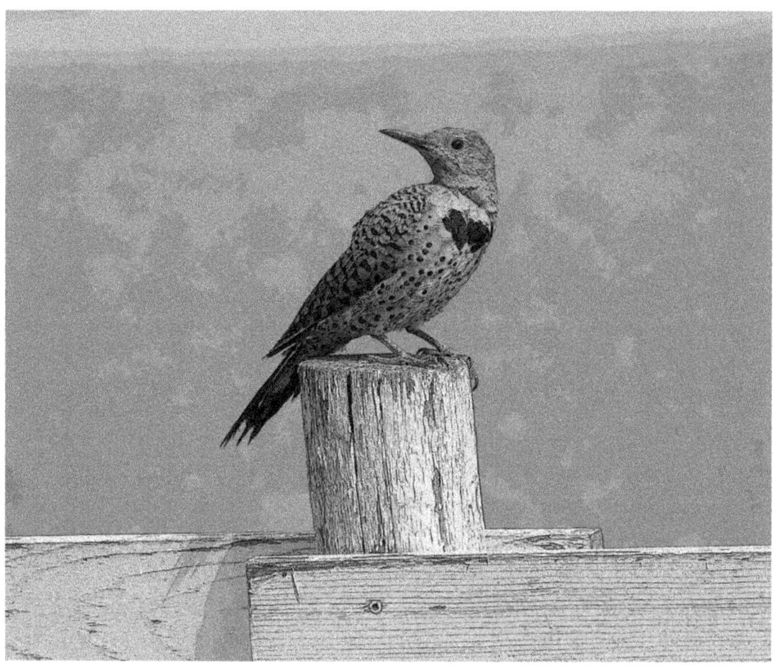

Male Northern Flicker Woodpecker

<h1 style="text-align:center">CHAPTER 7</h1>

Flip, Flop and Fly close by my eye

SOME OF THE DAY'S CROWS FLY FROM trees across the street swooping over the porch to us sitting there. It is like a sliding off of a slide coming at you. Only some days though! The House Sparrows are friendly, they fly into the porch and out the other end, just missing you. Sometimes they come right up onto the porch floor! Can't leave any spilled seed on the porch floor! You will have no privacy.

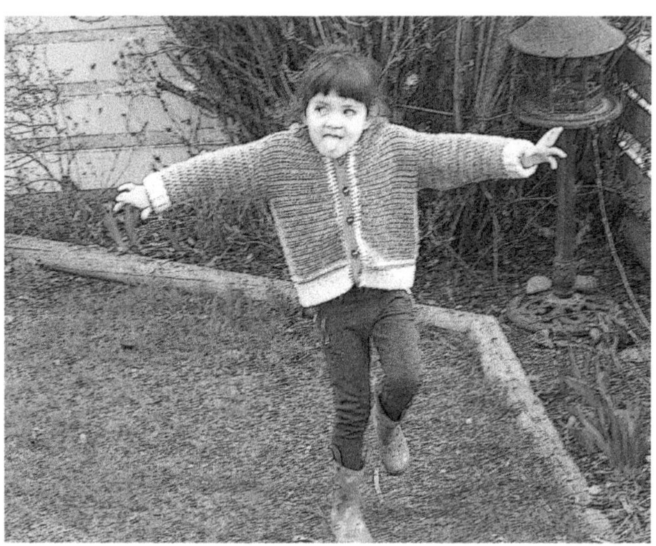

CHAPTER 8

Sometime Visitors

ONCE IN A WHILE THE PEREGRINE FALCON will fly into the yard and sit on the fence and look around. "They can watch you like a hawk!" As swift as a speeding arrow and more rapid than a cheetah, the peregrine falcon is the fastest member of the animal kingdom, with a diving speed of more than 200 miles per hour. The peregrine falcon is a well-respected falconry bird due to its strong hunting ability, high trainability, versatility, and availability via captive breeding - on a Training farm. The female looks more muscular than the male and, because of her greater bulk, her head can appear smaller relative to her body. The male has a smoother, sleeker appearance. The Falcons have big round eyes. The Falcon makes a shrill piecing cry.

Sometimes Aria wants to 'fly like eagle'. She knows the Falcon is hawk, so she is settled for being a Falcon. Aria tries to make the sound, but it just too high pitched. Angela asks, "Falcons catch the neighborhood pigeons?"

Aria would like to "Fly"

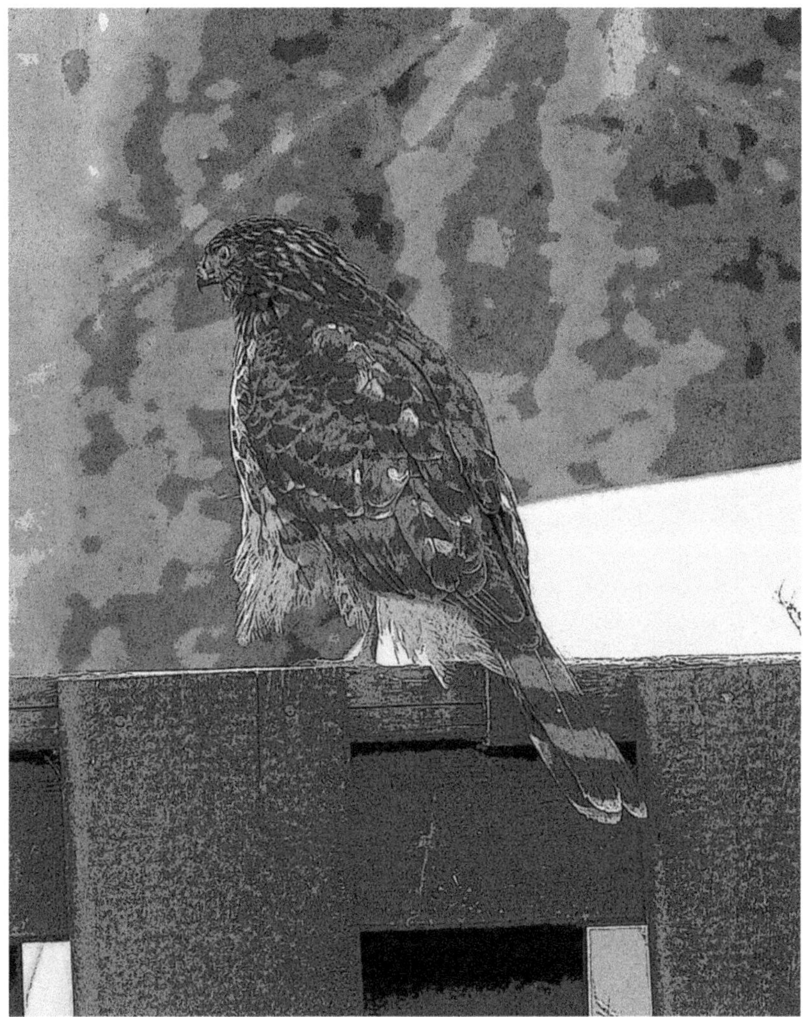

The Falcon

CHAPTER 9

Sometime Visitors with colorful feathers

SPOTTED TOWHEE - MALES HAVE JET-BLACK UPPERPARTS and throat; their wings and back are spotted bright white. The flanks are warm rufous and the belly is white. The female looks like the male but is not as bright colored. They are smaller than a robin.

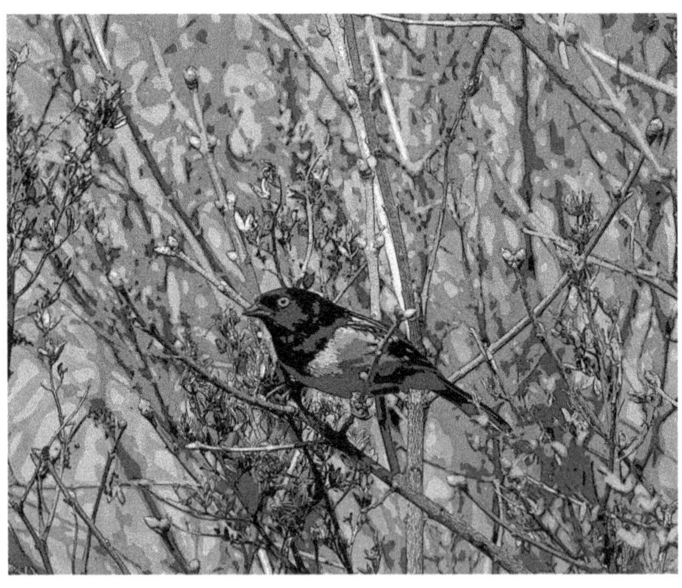

The Red winged Blackbird - The blackbird has an ok-ka-lee. It is loud! The song goes for 1-second starting with an abrupt note that goes into amelodic trill. It is another noisy one, but is alright as long as it does not stay for days, and days! If they come in the morning it is cheerful, and it will wake you up! These birds travel in large flocks.

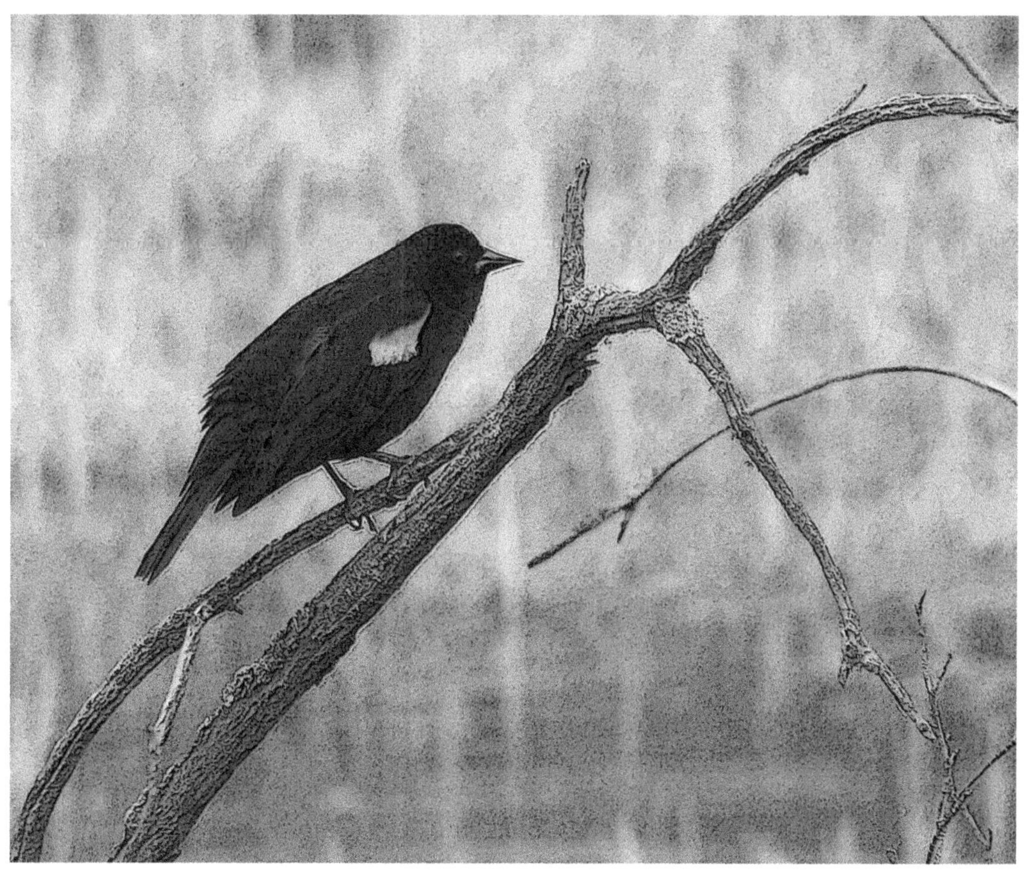

CHAPTER 10

Humming Birds

UMMING BIRDS ARE AMONG THE SMALLEST BIRDS, too, with most species measuring 3 to 5 inches long. The smallest bird, the bee hummingbird, is only 2 inches long—and weighs less than 2 grams. Hummingbirds, with their bright and many colors and fairly short wings, beat their wings as fast as 80 times per second! They do NOT flap their wings—they rotate them in a figure 8, which makes it even more remarkable! In fact, their name comes from the fact that they move their wings so fast that they make a humming noise. Hummingbirds can hover, stop instantly, and fly in different directions (even upside down) with exquisite control. In the spring, 21 species fly thousands of miles northward from Mexico, Costa Rica, and other southern places to visit the United States and Canada. In the fall, they return to their southern homes. "Grandma loves learning about all the birds that come into the yard," the kids noticed.

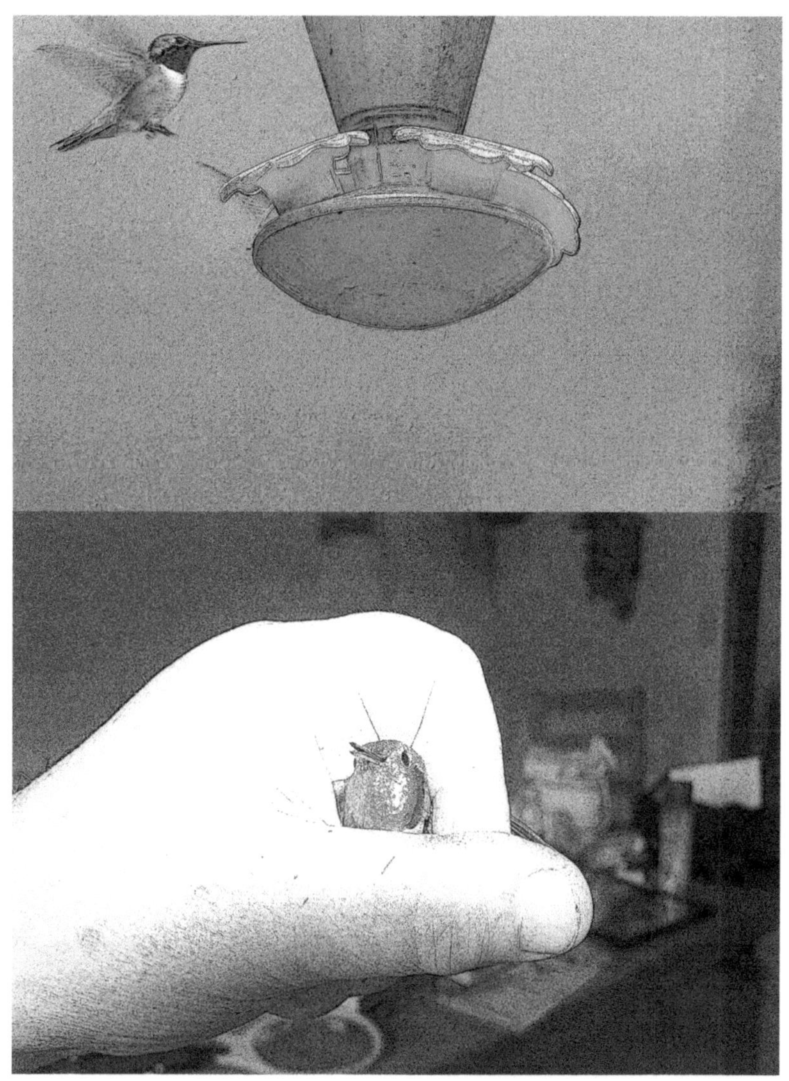

Humming bird in the creases of the human fingers

Chapter 11

Picnic Day on the Nature Island

GRANDMA IS DRIVING THE CHILDREN TO SCOUT Island. The Island is not far from downtown. The kids will get to see swans, ducks, the red winged black-bird again, and the beautiful white swan, and maybe see a beaver house? This is a real treat of nature for them! What a happy ending to the summer visit!

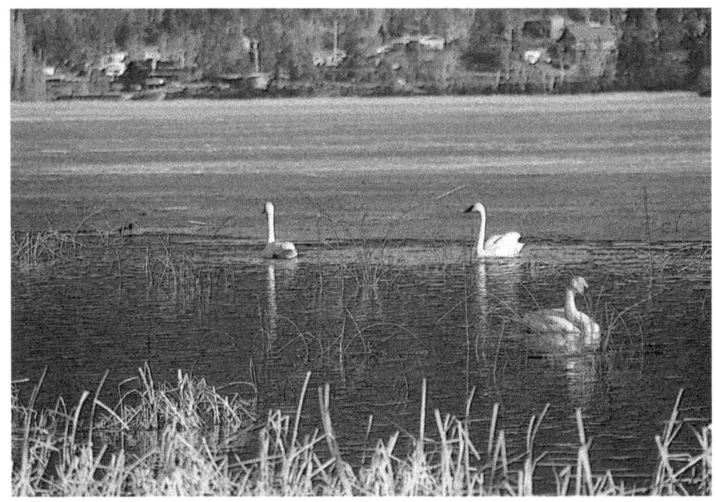

Trumpeter Swan

Bird Trivia

Male birds are more colorful than female birds.

Birds have more than one, each of a song or a squawk.

Birds have ears, the same as people – they are covered by feathers.

Birds do not have teeth – birds have gizzards.

Birds have feathers not fur.

Birds have 3 toes and a big toe.

Birds' nostrils opening is at the very end of their beak.

The name "house", like the House Sparrow, and the House Finch means they are sociable to humans.

Did you know?

Claws are on all *toes* to hold them when they perch on a branch.

Gizzards are a digestive system for a bird, and it is in the throat; it is a croak; which is a small stomach to gather food. A bird takes bugs & seeds, and eats tiny rocks to go to their stomach, which binds all of it up, and makes it soft. Birds have no teeth. Adults can feed this soft food their babies.

Plastic toy birds do not have gizzards, they cannot eat!

∞∞∞∞

About the Author

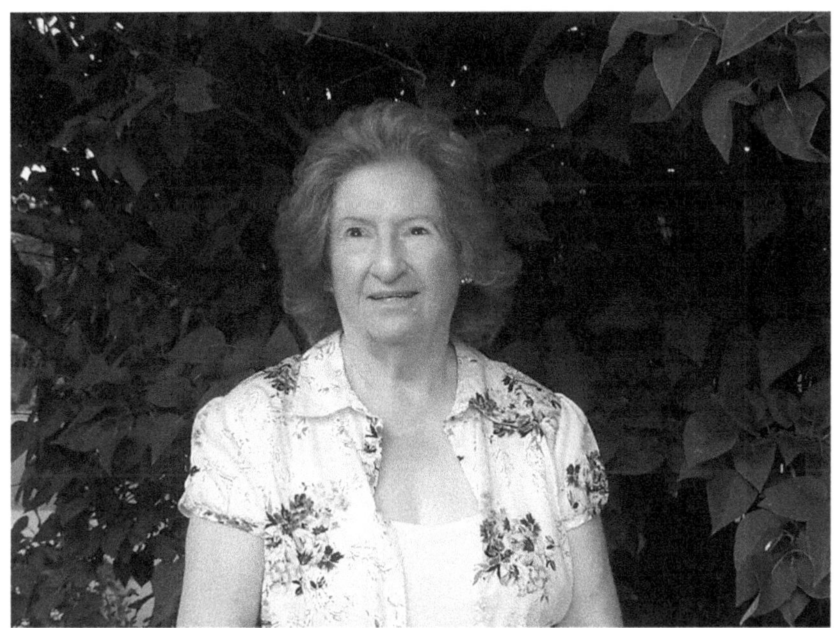

THE AUTHOR CONTINUES TO DO FREELANCE PHOTOGRAPHY and writing. Jessie is self taught and a self starter in many areas of her talents. Jessie Eldora Robertson is published on Online Photography stock sites: Shutterstock, Getty Images and Dreamstime. Published writing works include Anthologies in poetry books. She has edited her late husband's book - finally, in 2022: The Autobody Repair

Man by George L. Phillips. Published (to date) is her own Memoir, a revised edition * Best Edition - Working like A Man. Jessie's first Children's book is: Run Away and Hide: Hiding – featuring Little Aria. Published is – Little Missy Foodie: Kids Food Book.

Little Aria lives with the author, her (Great) Grammy Jessie, G. Granddad Bill and Mommy Brittany in the Cariboo Chilcotin in the city of Williams Lake, British Columbia, Canada.